Tails Are Not for Pulling

Elizabeth Verdick

Illustrated by Marieka Heinlen

free spirit
PUBLiSHiNG®

Helping kids
help themselves™
since 1983

Free Spirit, Free Spirit Publishing, and associated logos are trademarks and/or registered trademarks of Free Spirit Publishing Inc. A complete listing of our logos and trademarks is available at www.freespirit.com.

Library of Congress Cataloging-in-Publication Data
Verdick, Elizabeth.
    Tails are not for pulling / by Elizabeth Verdick ; Illustrated by Marieka Heinlen.
        p. cm.—(Best behavior series)
    ISBN 1-57542-181-X (pbk.)
1. Pets—Juvenile literature. I. Heinlen, Marieka, ill. II. Title. III. Series.
    SF416.2.V47 2005b
    636.088'7—dc22
                                                    2005013909

Cover and interior design by Marieka Heinlen

10 9 8 7 6 5 4 3 2
Printed in Hong Kong

Free Spirit Publishing Inc.
217 Fifth Avenue North, Suite 200
Minneapolis, MN 55401-1299
(612) 338-2068
help4kids@freespirit.com
www.freespirit.com

Dedication

This book is dedicated to my parents. Although they probably wouldn't describe themselves as pet lovers, they were kind enough to indulge my childhood passion for all things furry, and to let me adopt hamsters, cats, and one (very misunderstood) dog.
To my mom, who faithfully shopped for pet food and took my animals to all their vet appointments; and to my dad, who has never outgrown his enthusiasm for visiting zoos, wildlife centers, or animal sanctuaries throughout the world.
—E.V.

For Tiny and Milo, and for Patrick,
even though he isn't a "cat person."
—M.H.

Acknowledgments

We especially want to thank Becky Bishop, executive director of Reading With Rover, and veterinarian and "Animal Doctor" columnist Michael Fox, D.Sc., Ph.D., B.Vet.Med., MRCVS. We appreciate your expertise and encouragement!

Dear Parents and Caregivers,

Like many of you, I have pets I love. My family includes not only my husband and children, but also a small dog named Sunny, whose personality fits his name, two regal cats (Cleopatra and Zella), and a friendly, squeaky guinea pig called Gus. We share our home with these pets because they bring so many wonderful things to our lives: warmth, laughter, fun, and a bit of the unexpected. We once found Sunny standing on the kitchen table, where he had managed to eat someone's leftover snack but didn't know how to get down. We have watched Cleopatra parade along the side of the tub while the children are bathing, only to lose her balance and fall in with a big splash. And we have learned that our guinea pig will vibrate, chirp, and even do a "popcorn" dance of jumps and hops. Studies have shown that pets can help bring a smile to your face, as well as reduce anxiety and promote feelings of peace. More simply, pets can help us all learn to be more loving people.

　　If you're a parent who has animals in the home, a teacher with a classroom pet, or a therapist whose work includes a service dog, you have probably seen the magical moments that can happen between children and animals. It's heartwarming to see a child petting or hugging an animal while saying, "I love you." Or to watch as a child learns about the daily care and feeding of a pet. Or to observe as a child reaches out to an animal and becomes more motivated and builds new skills as a result. Caring, kindness, empathy, responsibility, and a respect for all living creatures—these are just a few of the things that animals help teach.

　　Tails Are Not for Pulling can help children understand that although animals may not have words, they communicate. Paying attention to an animal's cues—a joyful bark, a scary growl, a swishing tail—can help a child understand what the animal is "saying" and what an appropriate response may be. Most importantly, this book is about showing children how to love a pet gently—because pets are for loving, after all.

~Elizabeth

If pets could talk,
what do you think they'd say?

But what does
that mean?
Maybe . . .

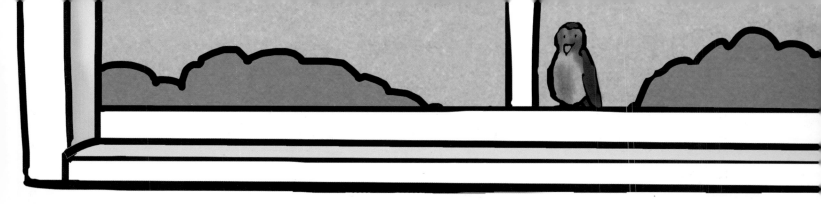

"Fur is for petting."

Not grabbing

5

"Ears are for listening."

Not yanking

If pets could talk,
what *else* do you think
they'd say? Maybe . . .

"Hey, my bowl is empty!"

12

Or . . .

"Gee, I could use a walk."

13

But most of all . . .

14

"Pets are for loving, not teasing."

What does
teasing look like?
It's when you . . .

hold my toys
out of reach

pretend to
take my food

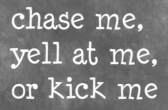

chase me,
yell at me,
or kick me

act like you
might hit me

17

What might teasing feel like?

It's
scary.

It's confusing.

I get mad.

I want to hide.

"It makes pets run away from me."

"It's not as fun as it seems."

"I feel bad after I tease."

What happens when you tease?

A pet may try to warn you:

20

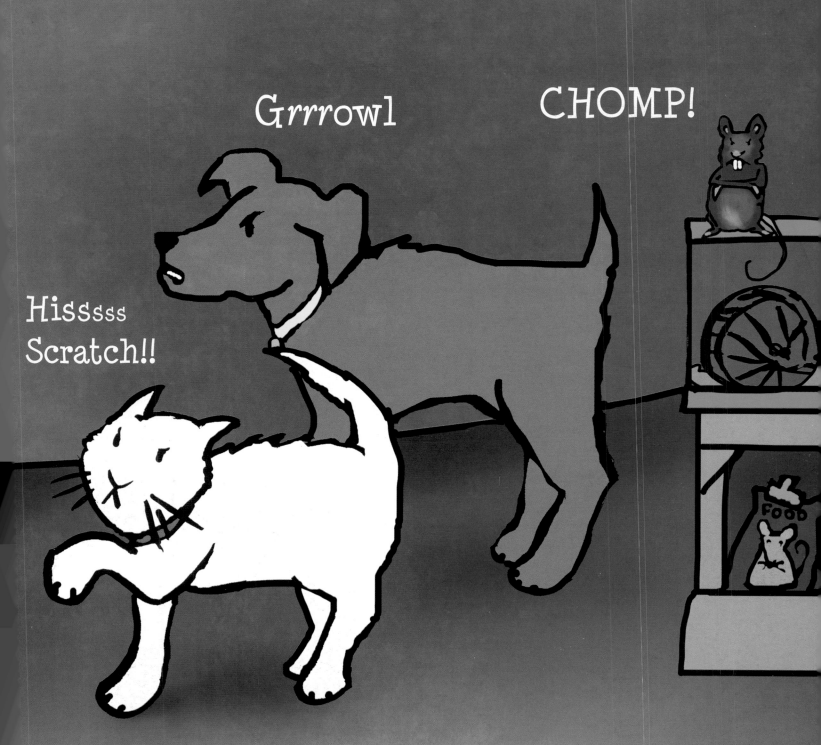

That's a pet's way of saying, "Hands off."

Whether they have fur, feathers, or fins, pets can feel things.

And pets can get hurt if you don't treat them well.

If you want to touch someone's pet,
here's one important rule:
Ask the person first.

"May I please
pet your pet?"

25

To show that you're an animal friend, you can reach your hand out slowly, talk to pets quietly, and touch them very gently.

Slowly, quietly, gently . . .

Purrrrrrr

You can love your pets from their heads down to their tails, but don't forget . . .

28

Tails are not for pulling—
they're for wagging!

Slurp!

29

Being a Friend to Animals

Critter Care

"Should My Child Have a Pet?"
(Some Answers for Parents)

Many parents struggle with this question, and it's especially tricky when you're looking into the eyes of a young child who's eager (and pleading) for a pet. Here are some thoughts to keep in mind:

- 🐾 **Observe your child interacting with other pets first.** Praise the positive interactions; gently correct the not-so-positive ones. Model how to pick up an animal, hold it carefully, and touch it gently. Make sure your child knows where on the body the pet accepts being touched.

- 🐾 **Think about starting small.** In general, larger animals require more care and live longer than smaller pets do, so an animal like a cat or a dog is a big commitment. Good starter pets for some families include goldfish or rodents.

- 🐾 **Choose wisely.** Getting a pet is a formative experience for children, and you'll want it to be as positive as possible. Think about your child's age, preferences, personality, and level of responsibility. What pet might truly be the best fit?

- 🐾 **Make sure the timing is right.** The holiday season is usually not a great time to bring home the newest member of your family. Try to pick a time when things are calmer and less rushed.

- 🐾 **Consider adoption.** So many wonderful animals are waiting in shelters for a family to come in and adopt them! And this includes not only cats and dogs, but also birds, guinea pigs, bunnies, hamsters . . . the list goes on.

- 🐾 **Research your options.** Many families are surprised to discover the expense and time commitment pets entail. Ask a local animal shelter or veterinarian for information, or check under Pet Adoption Information at the "Pets" Web page of the Humane Society of the United States (www.hsus.org/pets).

- 🐾 **Have a good backup plan.** Some families realize too late that their child has an allergy, or the pet they've chosen is sick, or they can't afford the extra expense of pet ownership. It's important to know ahead of time what you'll do if for some reason you can't keep the pet—and how you'll explain this to your child.

- 🐾 **Keep a watchful eye.** Don't assume that your child and the pet will always treat each other well. Young children need help learning how to show respect for animals, and how to recognize when an animal may be saying, "Hands off, please." If your child teases the pet, talk about how animals get scared or confused when they're mistreated. You might say, "Pets are our friends. Friends don't tease." For more about animal "talk," see page 33.

A Word About Unusual Pets

Hedgehogs, chinchillas, reptiles, amphibians, and tarantulas are fascinating, but creatures like these need special care, special diets—and special consideration before buying. There may be unforeseen housing and health concerns (for example, reptiles carry salmonella bacteria), as well as laws or regulations about owning exotic pets where you live. Never take in animals from the wild (instead, purchase domesticated pets born and bred in good facilities).

Kindness to Animals

All children—the youngest ones included—need to learn that animals are living, feeling beings. Even toddlers can understand that pets feel the difference between gentle and rough touches. Here are some ideas for modeling ways to handle a pet kindly:

For very young children, you can demonstrate on a stuffed animal, showing how to pet it slowly, quietly, and gently. In a group setting, you may want to ask an adult (for example, a parent or a therapist who works with a service animal) to bring a live pet to help give children a lesson in treating animals gently.

For children between the ages of two and three, you may want to take the lesson further by asking them to imagine what the pet feels. At this age, most children can begin to empathize in simple ways. They can relate to "Ouch, hitting hurts" or "Touch gently, please." They can imagine how a pet might feel if he or she is squeezed too tightly or dropped on the floor. Encourage young children to ask themselves: "Would *I* like it?"

For children ages four to six, you can suggest that they "put themselves in the pet's 'paws.'" How would it feel to be a pet that is pushed, pulled, poked, hit, kicked, or stepped on? Talk about kindness, fairness, and respect for living things. Around this age, many children are learning about the importance of treating others the way they want to be treated—and they can learn to apply this concept to animals as well as people. Because their understanding of fairness is growing, they can begin to talk about how pets deserve to be treated: with kindness, caring, and love.

Depending on the children's ages and maturity, they may (or may not) be ready to talk about why it's wrong to hurt animals. Use your own judgment about this. You could keep it as simple as, "It's not okay to hurt a pet." Or, go further by saying, "Animals have feelings too." Of course, that statement is open to interpretation, and you'll need to consider your own point of view. While most people agree that animals can feel pain or show fear as humans do, not all accept the idea that animals have feelings like happiness, sadness, or anger. On the other hand, some people believe very strongly that animals have feelings and deserve to be treated in a manner that honors that principle. Your own beliefs about this can guide how you teach the children in your care.

Children may naturally personify what a pet is feeling: "She's happy to see me," or "He's sad because we didn't feed him." At the same time, they may ask questions like, "Do animals get mad like people do?" or "Does a pet feel love?" You might answer with your own question: "What do you think?" Children often have their own answers, but are seeking reassurance or looking for a chance to share their views.

A Word About Animal Cruelty

Sadly, animal cruelty happens—but one of the most effective tools for preventing it is in your hands as a parent or an educator. Children who are taught about kindness and responsibility toward animals and all living creatures are learning one of life's most important lessons. They are more likely to treat animals humanely, to stick up for an animal that is being hurt, or to report potential incidents of animal neglect or harm.

With young children, you'll want to be careful about how you address this topic, as a little information can go a long way. Many children become very upset if they hear detailed stories about an animal that has been hurt. Instead, you may wish to limit the discussion to why it's important for animals to receive the proper care and to be treated with kindness.

Let older children know that, at times, some people are mean to animals—and that it's not okay. Also explain that sometimes people haven't yet learned the right way to treat an animal and may hurt the animal accidentally. Help children understand that they can tell a trusted adult (such as a parent, a teacher, a childcare provider, a babysitter, or another caregiver) if they see an animal that looks hurt or sick. Make sure children realize that it's not a good idea to try to help the animal *themselves*—the best and safest choice is always to go to a grownup for help.

Fur, Feathers, Fins, and Fun

Find fun facts.

If you have a pet, find some fascinating facts about the animal you've chosen and share those with your children. Here are a few to get you started:

- Hickory, dickory, dock—a **mouse** really *can* run up a clock! (Mice have sharp nails that help them cling to different surfaces.)

- **Parakeets** have two toes that point forward, and two that point backward.

- **Rabbits** can be trained to use a litter box. Some **cats** can be trained to use a toilet!

- **Cats** can make up to 100 vocal sounds. **Dogs** make about 10.

- A **dog's** sense of smell is about 1,000 times better than a person's. (And sometimes they enjoy the smells of things people think are pretty gross!)

- **Goldfish** are the most common household pet. And they've been kept as pets longer than any other kind of fish.

- Lizards and other reptiles such as **snakes** and **turtles** are cold-blooded. That means their body temperature changes as their environment gets hotter or colder.

- **Birds** have hollow bones so they're very light, which helps them to fly.

- A rodent's teeth are always growing. That's why **hamsters**, **gerbils**, **mice**, **rats**, and **guinea pigs** need to have wood to nibble on.

What do pets need?

Pets need what people need: food and water, a clean place to live, exercise, and sometimes medicine. But there's one other very important thing that pets need—and that's love. Talk to your children about these needs and why they matter. Ask them about ways we show love for an animal. Are there "right" ways and "wrong" ways? For example, do all pets enjoy hugs and kisses—why or why not? Have the children draw pictures of ways they show love for a favorite pet, and hang these works of art around the room.

"Happiness is a warm puppy."

(In the words of Charles Schulz, creator of the eminently lovable Snoopy.) Ask the children about ways our pets help make us feel happy. Examples: "My dog always greets me at the door and makes me feel welcome," or, "I feel so peaceful when I watch fish swimming in an aquarium." For fun, the children can draw pictures of the ways that animals help them feel good inside.

Pets have so much to give.

Talk about the special things that pets may bring to our lives. (They play with us when we're lonely, they help us feel comforted when we're sad, they're fun to watch, they make us laugh with the funny things they do—what else?) Ask each child to talk about an animal "friend" she or he has at home, in the classroom, or at the home of a friend or relative. What is that animal's name? How does it look? Why is it special?

Animal "Talk," Tales, and Tails

How do animals "talk"?

Throughout *Tails Are Not for Pulling,* the animals on the pages have many things to "say" about how they would like to be treated. But because animals can't speak using words, we have to teach children to listen to the many other ways that animals communicate. Ask children to come up with ways different animals use their "voices" (barking, meowing, growling, hissing, squeaking, chirping, whistling, purring, and more). What might these sounds mean? Demonstrate how a bark (or any other animal noise) could mean two very different things, depending on the situation. For example, some barks are joyful; some sound out a warning. Help children learn to distinguish the meanings of different sounds.

How do animals "talk" with their bodies?

Teach your children to tune in to the different cues animals may give us—even the cues we can't actually hear. Animal body language can give important clues about what the animal might do next. For example, a dog that is wagging her tail is probably excited and ready to play. But a cat that is switching his tail back and forth may be sending a very different message—like, "Back off." (A cat may also give a warning by arching his back, ruffling his fur, or puffing up his tail.) Help children understand this kind of body language so they're more aware of when it's okay—or not okay—to approach an animal. Be sure to give specific examples of how a specific pet may "talk" with the body, tail, ears, whiskers, nose, feathers, or nails.

When the teeth do the talking.

Even the gentlest pets have been known to bite or nip (or, for that matter, scratch). They may do this when they're excited, scared, or provoked—or simply by accident. Have first aid supplies handy so you can clean and dress the cut quickly. Let children know that "hurting the animal back" is never a good response. The National Association for Humane and Environmental Education (NAHEE) recommends reporting any bites to the local animal control. For tips on preventing bites, visit www.nahee.org/bite.asp.

Amazing-but-true tales.

We've all heard stories of amazing things animals have done. Some animals aid the police in solving crimes, or rescue people in life-threatening situations, or help people with special needs to live more independent lives. You can find books about animal heroes to read to children, or clip photographs and stories from magazines and newspapers. Share these inspiring tales so children can learn more about the important ways that animals help make the world a better place.

Amazing animal tails.

Show pictures of different animals, birds, fish, and reptiles so children can study the variety of tails. (You don't have to limit this activity to domestic animals—choose wild animals as well, if you'd like.) Which one has the longest tail? The shortest? The curliest? The straightest? The most colorful? The prettiest? The goofiest? Find some fun facts about animal tails to share. (Example: A mouse's tail is the same length as its body. Mice use their tails for balance when they run or stand up on their hind legs.) Talk about the many different ways that tails "talk": by wagging, waving, wiggling, swishing, bristling, ruffling, dragging—what else?

For more on tails, check out:

Tails That Talk and Fly by Diane Swanson (Vancouver, BC: Greystone Books, 1999). Whether they're flying, swimming, or "talking," tails have much to teach us.

What Do You Do with a Tail Like This? by Robin Page, illustrated by Steve Jenkins (Boston: Houghton Mifflin, 2003). This book talks about tails and the amazing—and weird—things that critters' other body parts can do. Children will learn, for instance, that a lizard can break off its tail as a defense—and that the tail will grow back!

About the Author and Illustrator

Elizabeth Verdick is the author of several award-winning books in the Best Behavior™ series for young children, including *Words Are Not for Hurting, Teeth Are Not for Biting,* and *Feet Are Not for Kicking.* She is the coauthor (with Marjorie Lisovskis) of *How to Take the Grrrr Out of Anger* and has coauthored several books with Trevor Romain, including *Stress Can Really Get on Your Nerves!* She is the coauthor (with Pamela Espeland) of the Adding Assets Series for upper elementary-age students, *Dude, That's Rude!,* and *Making Every Day Count.* Elizabeth has edited more than 30 books for children, teens, and adults. She lives with her husband, daughter, and son near St. Paul, Minnesota.

Marieka Heinlen is the illustrator of the award-winning Best Behavior series of books for young children that includes *Words Are Not for Hurting, Teeth Are Not for Biting, Feet Are Not for Kicking,* and *Hands Are Not for Hitting.* As an art director she designs and illustrates books and other materials for children, teens, parents, and teachers. She lives in St. Paul, Minnesota.

Fast, Friendly, and Easy to Use
www.freespirit.com

Browse the catalog   Info & extras   Reliable resources   Many ways to search   Quick check-out   Stop in and see!

To place an order or to request a free catalog of SELF-HELP FOR KIDS® *and* SELF-HELP FOR TEENS® *materials, please write, call, email, or visit our Web site:*

Free Spirit Publishing Inc.
217 Fifth Avenue North • Suite 200 • Minneapolis, MN 55401-1299
toll-free 800.735.7323 • local 612.338.2068 • fax 612.337.5050
help4kids@freespirit.com • www.freespirit.com